MW01601587

How to Start an Office Cleaning Business

Judy Goode

Copyright © 2023 Judy Goode

All rights reserved.

No part of this book may be reproduced in any form or by any electronic or mechanical means, including information storage and retrieval systems, without written permission from the author, except for the use of brief quotations in a book review.

Visit me at GoodesCleaning.com

ISBN: 978-1-7365989-1-7

Disclaimer

This book is represented as information. It is not a business plan or business advice in any way. The success referred to in this book is the author's own personal experience. There are absolutely no warranties, liabilities, or guarantees referred to, expected, or implied in regards to this book, or the information therein.

DEDICATION

I dedicate this book to everyone who
reads it. May you too be very, very
successful. God bless your new
cleaning business.

CONTENTS

ACKNOWLEDGMENTS

First and foremost, to God for giving me the wherewith all, when times were tough, for giving me good health to keep things going, for giving me the spirit of gratitude, and most of all for giving me his love and never-ending blessings.

To my wonderful husband Andy who is such a strong and great supporter. I thank you for so many, many things that you have contributed to our cleaning company over the last 18 years. Your hands-on approach insisting that we clean with integrity to reflect your last name was the beginning of Goode's Cleaning services.

Andrew the most important lesson I learned from you was that we have no competition with other cleaning companies. Your pure wisdom that there is enough business to go around for everyone gave me the understanding that the ocean is full of water. Thank you for all you have done, for all you have given, and for all of your scarifies to help me make this a great and successful business. I love you always.

To my daughter Tee for all the years of sound advice, and for your great help in the last edition of editing this book. Thank you for helping me so much with this book. To all the years of your great moral support and constant love. I love you so much.

To my four wonderful grandchildren Shannel, Shadear, Shamina, and A J who all helped out throughout our early years, Thank you.

To all my employees over the last 18 years, I say thank you. Each and every one of you have contributed to our success. I especially want to thank Jenny Mullins who has been with me for over 15 years through thick and thin, thank you Jenny for your loyalty and great service to Goode's Cleaning.

To all of our wonderful loyal customers throughout all these years, All of us at Goode's Cleaning say thank you for trusting us with your homes and offices.

To Beth Mynatt for encouraging me to just go ahead and write this great book, thank you Beth for pushing me on.

To Dr. Wendy Norfleet my great coach throughout this book, I thank you for accepting the challenge, I thank you for your great patience chapter per chapter I also thank you for never giving me any doubts that I could do this. Wendy, I am looking forward to writing many more books, thank you.

To Kim Deppe who told me many years ago to go ahead and write this book. Thank you, Kim, for editing my book. Your confidence in me meant the world.

To BNI my very first networking group, thank you for all the knowledge I acquired your "Givers Gain" philosophy is a lesson every entrepreneur needs to understand. Your encouragement and one-on-one meetings with one another truly are one of the marks of excellence well taught in your meetings.

To my Beautiful BIZ NET Family

network group in Orange Park Fl. Over the last 12 years, I have dedicated my business to being part of this phenomenal weekly meeting group whose 50 members are all experts in their services, and whose 50 members are dedicated to helping one another with great referrals. Thank you, Biz Net, for all the trust you have given me over the years with your referrals.

To Finally Friday, one of the greatest, most friendliest networking groups I have the pleasure to attend once a week. Thank you for embracing me over the last 9 years.

To The Jacksonville Chamber of Commerce and to The Clay Chamber of Commerce, thank you.

To Mark Carillion who encourage me to go on Google.

To Angie's List for the Super Service Awards for so many years. Thank you.

1: MY STORY – MEET THE FOUNDER

Hello, my name is Judy Goode and I am the owner of Goode's Cleaning Services, Inc. founded in June 2004. We are a Christian-based firm. Our level of integrity is extremely high. We know that God is always watching us. Our Love for Christ sets us apart and that's why......

We Don't Cut Corners We Clean Them!

I have been married to Andy for 53 years. We have a lovely daughter, four grandchildren, and five great-grandchildren. For 34 years I spent my career as a Wall Street Computer Director, managing over 30 employees. After the attack on the

World Trade Center on September 11, 2001, I was afraid to commute into New York City. My husband Andy and I decided to retire from our careers. We sold our home in New Jersey in 2003 and decided to move to the beautiful and sunny state of Florida. For one full year, we perfected the art of doing nothing, which was a lot of fun. However, it was time to make the doughnuts and we knew that we wanted to do something together. So, I decided to look for a cleaning job. I spoke to a big box franchise home cleaning company and they could not accommodate the part-time hours I wanted. So, I went home and googled how to start a cleaning company. I chose an ad that charged $39.00 for their eBook. Well, that was the best $39.00 I ever spent. I opened up Goode's Cleaning Services In 2004. We now have over 20 employees and service over 200 homes and about 50 offices. This is why 18 years later, I too am charging you $39.00. May your $39.00 also be the best investment you make.

In 2008, the Jacksonville Chamber of Commerce nominated our cleaning company Small Business Leader of the Year. In 2014, the Clay County Chamber of Commerce awarded us Business of the month. Additionally, Angie's List, a nationally renowned organization, has awarded us the Super Service Award for the years 2014 thru 2020. We are so honored that WJXT Channel 4 "Look Local" aired an interview on Goode's Cleaning in May 2018. This interview is available on www.goodescleaning.com

2: THE TIME IS NOW: ARE YOU READY? LET'S GO!

Today, you have made a great decision and investment. This investment in the future is the gift that will keep on giving because once you get a customer as long as you continue to give them great quality service you can count on their revenue every single month. The fact that the customers you obtain will want your services either weekly, bi-weekly, or monthly will create an ongoing stream of income.

This security of income allows you to sleep well at night.

The excitement that I have for you and your future cleaning business is tremendous.

This manual is my tried and proven success guide of how I started my cleaning company and how I have maintained both customers and employees over the last 18 years.

This manual will guide you to become one of the Best Cleaning companies in your area.

Cleaning offices is a service that is easy to do and will always be needed. Companies are always in need of maintaining a clean environment for the safety and health of their entire company.

In the era of COVID-19, the cleaning requirements have become more and more essential.

My guide throughout this manual will get you ready to start

immediately so that you can reap the financial rewards.

Cleaning is an industry that generates over $61 billion every year in America.

Your chances of obtaining offices to clean are really very good.

Most small businesses prefer a small company that allows them to speak directly to the owner, rather than a franchise.

It is very important that every time you get a new customer you tell them you want them to share anything that might displease them. Tell them their feedback will help you keep the level of your services high.

In the beginning, I recommend you clean the offices yourself, to build trust with your customer. However, if you don't want to do any of the cleaning yourself and you just want to be a boss, I encourage you to hire someone who you personally know, preferably an individual who you feel is going to do a great job and someone who will represent you well. Remember these are your first customers, you MUST - I repeat you MUST - treat your new business with kid gloves. As you grow the business, I strongly suggest that you work hand in hand and train your new employees yourself. This method of success will be a huge asset to your business growth. Make sure that the individual you train mirrors your image exactly how you show them to clean.

Right at the start, explain to your employee the importance of cleaning ONLY the way you teach them. Remind them this is your business and your reputation, and as long as they work for you, they must do it your way. Always call the customer after your first cleaning to make sure they were pleased.

Ask the customer if there is anything they would like you to do differently?

NOTES

_____

_____

_____

_____

_____

_____

_____

_____

_____

_____

_____

_____

3: AFFORDABLE BUDGET

This book will guide you through setting up a successful office cleaning business. A business, by the way, that can sustain you.

A successful office cleaning business can be started with less than $400.00 dollars. Yes, you read right - less than $400.00. When you first start, you need to make a small investment to get your business started. You may need a business license for about $50 (not all communities or cities require this). You will need business insurance, amounts can vary. I recommend you get a policy for one hundred thousand dollars. This small amount will enable you to pay a small upfront $200 down payment and pay a small monthly payment. When

I bought my eBook, it was recommended not to buy the insurance right away. I was encouraged to wait until a customer asked me for it. Business cards can be quite inexpensive. For less than $25.00, you can have cards made online and delivered to you. A printer is not a must but is sold at big box stores for less than $75.00. Paper is less than $5.00 a ream. Use paper for your flyers. (Sample template provided at the end of Chapter 14.) Cleaning products can cost you less than $20.00 and office supplies about the same. You may already have some of these items on hand.

I want to ask you a million-dollar question: do you like to clean? It is important to take a moment to think about this question. Even if your answer is no, but you do not mind cleaning or you're good at it, then this is the business for you. Taking a moment to reflect on this question is essential because when you first start, either you will be doing the cleaning yourself or, you hire someone and you have a great responsibility to train them.

Keep in mind what I am providing you is, in essence, like a cake recipe...a recipe with ingredients and instructions. If you want the same results that I achieved, you must follow the recipe.

Now let's talk more about the formula for success.

The first thing I am providing you with is a list of potential customers that will become your future clients.

You will find these businesses, typically at many shopping plazas or at corporate business parks.

NOTES

_____

_____

_____

_____

_____

_____

_____

_____

_____

_____

_____

_____

4: HOW TO GET CUSTOMERS

I am providing you with a list of potential customers that will become your future clients. Note the list below has many categories for you to get customers.

- Acupuncturists
- Banks
- Business Offices
- Cardiologist
- Car Dealer Showrooms
- Chiropractors
- Certified Public Accountants
- Day Care Centers
- Dentists
- Dermatologist
- Doctor's Offices
- Electrical Repair
- Family Medical Centers

- Fitness Centers
- Gastroenterologist
- GYN and Obstetrician
- Hair Salons
- Internal Medicine
- Insurance Offices
- Law Firms
- Massage Therapists
- Medical Offices
- Mobile Phone Stores
- Opticians/Optometrists
- Physical Therapists
- Plumbing Companies
- Podiatrists
- Psychiatrist
- Radiologist
- Real Estate Agencies
- Spas

NOTES

_____

_____

_____

_____

_____

_____

_____

_____

_____

_____

_____

_____

5: REFERENCES

When I started, my first client asked for references. Unfortunately, I did not know any of this information that I am sharing with you. Once I gave my first client the price, he asked for a reference. Being new, I told him that I did not have a reference. He said, "Forget it, you are not going to use me as a guinea pig!" I quickly asked if he would allow me to clean his office for free?, stating that if he was happy with my services, he would pay me and if not, he at least had a clean office. This is a technique that I highly recommend for anyone just starting out in the office cleaning business.

I recommend that you offer a few free cleanings to customers in order to use them as references.

When you identify your list of potential customers, you are going to want to knock on doors, introduce yourself, and let people know that you have a cleaning business. Now your true work begins. Take pride that you are the owner, take pride that you are going to do a great job in service to others, and never shy from telling your potential customers that you will work hard to provide quality service and earn their trust.

Another Source of Referral from Family and Friends

Most of our friends and family go to their doctors, their specialist, and their dentist, or even pay their phone bills in person, at their mobile carrier.

As you review the list of potential customers, I recommend that you call friends and relatives and ask for the name of the offices they visit. Inform them you are not looking for a referral, you just want names of local places that you can reach out to on your own.

These offices may already have someone who performs their cleaning, and that's ok because these become what are known in the industry as a lead. A lead is a company name that someone gives you. Your job is to follow up and call the company immediately to see if they can use your service. There are two types of leads. The first lead example is a Hot lead.

This hot lead means that a company is looking for help right away. Ask the person who gave you the lead if you can use their name as a referral. If they say no when you call the company just mention "I understand that you need someone to clean your office". The second lead is called a warm lead. For example, the company is using someone to clean the office. Your job is to call the company and ask the number one question: Are you pleased with your current cleaning company? Your objective is to stay in touch with this lead.

With the knowledge they already have a cleaning person, you can take control of the conversation.

Ask are you currently pleased with their service? If they say yes, they are pleased. Ask for permission to stay in touch and check with them as a follow-up call every 3 months. Never give up.

You will be amazed how status

can change from having help to needing new help. Trust me on this one! By following up periodically when the need for new help arises, you will be the first one they call.

Additionally, offering a free cleaning can help you develop some references. This method of offering a free cleaning enables you to ask can you use them as a reference.

Future clients can also be obtained through networking. When I started, I did not know the power of networking. I have an entire section on this topic.

Always remember your integrity is on display, be mindful of how you speak to people. This will play a very important role in their perception of you.

Never be rude or obnoxious to

someone who has been rude to you. Allow the Golden Rule to be your guide. "Do unto others as you would have them do unto you."

NOTES

_____

_____

_____

_____

_____

_____

_____

_____

_____

_____

_____

_____

6: BUSINESS SECRETS

Secret 1 – Contracts

Let your potential prospect know that they do not need to sign a contract. Tell them they only need to sign a mutual 30-day agreement. Explain that a 30-day agreement is for both parties because if either one of you wants to terminate this written agreement, you agree to give one another a 30-day notice. This level of confidence on your behalf becomes a great asset.

Give the customer the option to use your services on a **weekly, bi-weekly, monthly, or on an as-needed basis**.

Secret 2- Follow-up

You must, must, must call your customer the next day after you clean. Do not call before 11:00 am because you want to give them a chance to get in the office and allow them to do their own walkthrough.

It's important to ask if they had a chance to look over the cleaning job and if they are pleased.

Secret 3 – Accountability

Make sure you and your customer know that no one is perfect, Therefore, make sure you tell your client that if they see anything, and stress anything, that displeases them to please call you and you will make it right.

Secret 4 – Stay in Touch

Periodically stay in touch with potential clients by following up with a phone call every three months. This will help them remember who you are and give you a chance to ask if you can pay them a visit to meet them. Meeting them will become a great marketing tool. Explain the reason it's important for them to meet you in spite of not needing you at this time, is if in the future their needs were to change, they will feel like they already know who you are.

This is so crucial to building a relationship with a potential customer. I received new customers with this meeting technique. I offered to meet them at their office and did a five-minute walkthrough. Granted, sometimes it may take a while, but when their status changed, my name and number were at their fingertips. The fact that they met me previously meant they felt like they already knew me.

Secret 5 - Offer a Free Cleaning

The free cleaning will showcase your great quality. This is always helpful for those potential clients who are either not sure if they want and/or need a cleaning service.

Secret 6 – Keys

Never put a customer's address on a key tag. Inform the customer that for their safety, only their first name will appear on the key, in the event a key is lost.

Secret 7 - Door

This tip will make or break you......Always check the door when you are done. After locking the door, double-check that it is truly locked. Your worst nightmare is for the customer to call you the next morning and say you left their office unlocked. This happened to one of my employees, and we were lucky they gave us another chance.

Secret 8 – Phone Number

Always ask the customer for their

cell number. This is important, especially in the event of any emergency. You will have their number.

Secret 9 – Network

This is the most effective way to grow your business. More on this topic when you read the network chapter.

Secret 10 – Gratitude

Develop a spirit of thankfulness and gratefulness daily. This magical attitude will bring you much success.

NOTES

_____

_____

_____

_____

_____

_____

_____

_____

_____

_____

_____

_____

_____

7: CUSTOMER TIPS

There are many tips that I would like to offer you. However, keep in mind that you may think of some that are not included.

Tip 1 – Free Offer
Another free offer can be (for example) to clean the office and if they are not pleased, they get a free cleaning.

Tip 2 – Price
If someone says your price is too high, ask what is in their budget? Then, meet their price. This truly works.

Tip 3 – Flyers
Create colorful flyers that stand out when you give them to potential clients. Make sure your phone

number is included.

Tip 4 – Soliciting

When handing out flyers at corporate parks if you see a "no soliciting" sign you have two options. On a pad, write the office name and number and mail them the flyer, or walk inside and politely ask for their fax number and fax the flyer. This option is more cost-effective. (Note - not everyone has a fax, they might want you to email the information to them)

Tip 5 – Call

You can also just call and introduce your cleaning service and see if they need one. If they don't, get their fax number (or email address) and fax or email a flyer for their future needs.

Tip 6 – Door Chutes

A lot of offices have mail chutes

on their doors. This is an easy way to just put your flyer, business card, or both inside the mail chute.

Tip 7 – Alarms

For offices that have alarms, request they assign you the last 4 digits of your phone number as your code. This is really important as you don't want to get blamed for not turning on the alarm if someone else entered. It also gives your client a sense of security that they will always know when you are in the office.

Tip 8 – Frequency

Sometimes potential customers have never considered having a professional clean their office. Suggest to them to start once a month for a very affordable price. This suggestion helps because some may think that they have to sign up for a weekly commitment.

Tip 9 – "No"

You will sometimes find that when you speak to a potential customer they often may say no, but if the person they are using messes up they will pick up the phone and call you. So, remember a NO now does not mean a NO forever.

Tip 10 – Keys

Put customer's door key on a lanyard key chain and keep it around your neck. Sometimes doors slam lock, and you will get locked out, I know from experience

NOTES

_____

_____

_____

_____

_____

_____

_____

_____

_____

_____

_____

_____

8: HOW TO PRICE

When I bought my eBook, I was told to charge $45.00 to clean an office. So, the first customer who asked me how much it would cost to clean his office, I immediately, with confidence, said $45.00. The lawyer said "What are you crazy! That's too much money." I was scared and shocked that the price was not what he wanted. Only God put these next words in my mouth. "Sir, how much would you like to pay?" He said $25.00. I said okay, I will do it for $25.00. He said, "Wait a minute, do you have any experience? Do you have any references?" When I said NO, he said, "Never mind." By the grace of God, I said, "How about I clean your office and if you are happy with my cleaning, you pay me. If you are not happy you get your office cleaned for free."

Ladies and gentlemen, I never looked back. I cleaned his office and had my first customer and a referral for other customers. I was so happy! I got my first customer in less than two weeks. So can you!

The story I shared with you is important. No price is etched in stone. Always be open-minded to asking what are you looking to pay. You are new to the business. You need customers. You need references. So, in the beginning, you may have to use some common sense to get your new business going.

- The prices I list can vary from state to state.
- The prices can vary on the size of the office.
- The price can vary from all

carpets to all tiles.
- The price can vary from daily, weekly, bi-weekly, or monthly.

If the office is cleaned once a week, you can quote, for example, $45.00 per cleaning. If they want it cleaned bi-weekly, the price can be $55.00 per visit. If they want the office cleaned once a month, you can price it at $65.00

$45.00 Price

The most common small office in some corporate parks. This office can be cleaned weekly or bi-weekly. It will have one bathroom and about 3 – 4 small private offices. The floors are all carpeted except the bathroom and kitchen.

$65.00 Price

The office is all of the above, adding two bathrooms, a large conference room, a bigger breakroom (kitchen), and 5 – 6 more offices.

$100.00 Price

The office is all of the above and has 8 small offices. The entire office is tiled, which requires sweeping and mopping, and will always take you longer to finish.

A great going pricing rate is about $0.26 to $0.46 per square foot. A great example is to take total square footage divided by total price to get the per square footage.

The prices I have above will allow you great flexibility to lower the price whenever you need to. Remember my story where I lowered the price to $25.00 from the original $45.00, and I got my first customer? Do not be afraid to ask what they are currently paying to clean the office.

NOTES

_____

_____

_____

_____

_____

_____

_____

_____

_____

_____

_____

_____

9: COACHING SERVICE AVAILABLE TO YOU

When I bought my eBook, I wish I had the ability to call someone as additional questions came up.

For a small coaching fee of $99.00, you can have access to me to answer your questions and provide guidance. This fee includes two 30-minute sessions. In the beginning stages of your new business, I recommend registering for a minimum of one month to receive assistance in building your new business. This service is a great extension of the eBook and the video. In the event you have questions on how to handle a cleaning situation, how to reach out to a potential client, or something as simple as a comparison of cleaning products, the coaching fee is well worth its value. You can call, email, or text me with your questions.

You can subscribe now if you didn't take advantage of the offer when you brought your eBook.

Just go to our website www.goodescleaning.com and sign up now.

NOTES

_____

_____

_____

_____

_____

_____

_____

_____

_____

_____

_____

_____

_____

10: DEVELOPING RELATIONSHIPS

People always like doing business with who they know, who they like, and who they can trust. These are the rules for developing a business relationship.

Listed below are some things to consider as you build your business relationships.

- Be respectful.
- Be courteous.
- Be mindful of what you say.
- Keep your personal business to yourself.
- Have a great attitude both in person and on the phone.
- Never be argumentative (especially if you disagree).

- Be a great listener.
- Ask how you may improve the previous service.
- Invite other business owners for a coffee meeting (More on this in the Networking chapter.)
- Never take anything, from any office this includes paper clips, candy food, drinks, paper, products, and money.
- Always try to add value to your service. For example, point out something extra that you will clean at no extra charge like disinfect phones, doorknobs, or light switches.

NOTES

_____

_____

_____

_____

_____

_____

_____

_____

_____

_____

_____

_____

_____

11: HOW TO CULTIVATE PHONE CONVERSATIONS

Back in the 1970s, we used to say "let your fingers do the walking." This was a slogan used by the phone company when people looked in the yellow pages, a phone directory, to find a phone number. Today we use Google to find phone numbers and contacts. I recommend you make phone calls Tuesday through Thursday to prospective clients. In my experience, Monday and Friday's clients are usually not as receptive. Mondays they are busy getting their week started and Fridays they are wrapping up the week and ready to start the weekend. Call on a prospective client in place of knocking on their door. I promise you can make more calls sitting down in the comfort of your home per day than you can walk.

Every night before you go to sleep, visualize and concentrate on how wonderful tomorrow will be. Hear yourself saying "sure, what time would you like for me to come and give you a price for cleaning your office?"

When I worked in sales years ago we were encouraged to treat our daily sales calls as a numbers game. Decide early on how many calls you will make daily; my friendly suggestion is to make 25 calls. This magic number will keep you on track to actually speak to at least 10 people. You will find that from the 25 calls some people may be out to lunch or absent for the day. Others may not be able to come to the phone etc. Always create a mentally friendly mindset before you get on the phone. It helps to smile when speaking on the phone.

Every time you dial a number, be optimistic that they need your help.
Ask to speak to the office manager, and if they are out of the office request their name and call back asking for them by name.

Ask for permission to check periodically in case their status changes.

Request their fax number or email address to provide them with your flyer.

No matter how discouraged you become, remember that there is a yes out there waiting for you.

Phone Conversations Examples: Yes

Good morning (afternoon) My name is _____ with _____ cleaning company. May I speak to the office manager?

Hi, Office manager (use their name). My name is _____ and I have a cleaning service. We take a lot of pride in doing a great job - not once in a while, but every single visit.

Question: Do you currently have your office cleaned?

If they say Yes follow up with the next question.

Are you pleased with your current company?

If the answer is yes you reply:

Well, that's great! I would appreciate it if you allow me to fax or email my company information (your flyer and sample letter) in the event your future status changes.

Thank you. (end of conversation) Create a list of names of companies that you emailed or faxed your flyer and sample letter.

Phone Conversation Examples: No

Do you currently have your office cleaned? If the answer is no to the question above, your reply can be:

With everyone's health concerns about Covid 19, I would like to set up a ten-minute appointment with you to share not only how affordable my cleaning service is, but how important it has become to maintain a clean environment.

If they say no to the 10-minute

appointment, ask may I fax or email you some information in the event your status changes in the future? Don't forget to ask for the email address or fax number.

Thank you have a good day.

Different Conversation Examples

I would love to earn your business. May I come and visit your office?

If they say no,

1. Say I just would like to meet you with no obligations. Then in the event, your status were to change in the future, you will have my number and feel like you're not talking to a stranger.

2. I understand that at this time you don't need a new service, however with your permission may I stay in touch periodically in case your status changes?

3. May I give you a free estimate with no obligation on your behalf?

4. If there was something you would like to improve from your current service what would that be?

5. Would you consider letting us clean on Wednesday to compare our quality?

NOTES

_____

_____

_____

_____

_____

_____

_____

_____

_____

_____

_____

_____

12: LICENSE, INSURANCE, AND BONDING INFORMATION

As soon as I made the decision to create my cleaning company I immediately thought of a name for my company. The real easy name suggestion is either your first or last name. An example, I used my last name - Goode's Cleaning. I went online to my state to confirm that the name I had selected was not being used by another business company. Once I acquired my business name I went to IRS.Gov to get a Federal Tax ID number for my company.

I went to the bank with my Fed Tax ID number, and business documents to open up my bank account. I chose to do this because I wanted to keep my personal business account separate from my new business.

However, you can choose to start small and ask your customer to make your checks payable to you. As you grow, you can make other business decisions later. You can use your social security number instead of a Tax ID number.

I recommend you get a business license immediately; you must renew your license every year. To obtain a license go to your local county tax collector and register. There typically is a small fee. Not every town, city, or county requires a license, but it is better to know upfront what is required.

Once you have obtained some regular customers, you will want to invest in liability and bonding insurance. These insurances like the business license require yearly renewals.

Liability insurance is important to acquire in the event you or an employee break something of value, you can then file a claim. I additionally recommend that you create a small fund in the future, about $200.00 up to $500.00, to replace items that are not as valuable. This recommendation is important to consider in place of filing a small liability claim. Bonding insurance is the least expensive, it cost less than $200.00 per year. Bonding insurance is only used when a customer accuses you or an employee of yours, of stealing something. The burden of proof is always on the accuser, unless they saw the person steal or have a video proving the theft it's very hard for the accuser to win the case.

There may be two options to purchase insurance. 1. Purchase your insurance immediately, or save on expenses 2. You can choose to buy liability insurance and bonding insurance when your first customer requests it. Call a local agent, and visit their office to pay your deposit and sign some documents. You immediately will leave with your new company insured. In the future when a customer requests proof of insurance your agent can fax or email a copy both to you and your new customer.

NOTES

_____

_____

_____

_____

_____

_____

_____

_____

_____

_____

_____

_____

_____

13: OBTAINING PART-TIME HELP

Initially, you may be able to clean all the offices yourself, but what happens as your business grows? At first, you can get your spouse, kids, best friend, and others to help. The people you will choose to represent your cleaning business must be people that you trust. I do not recommend you hire help in the early days until you are savvy enough to make a good employee selection. Once you are ready for an employee you may purchase applications at an office supply store. Your applicant needs to complete an application, and you should check their references. Keep in mind, that the people who work for you represent your business and if they steal or damage property, you may lose a client.

Be prepared when you have a big office or suite of offices to clean, you either have to get help or ask for extended access time to clean the offices.

When I obtained my first big cleaning job, I asked for access to the offices from 6 pm on Friday to 6 am on Monday. Remember when I started, I was doing all the cleaning with my husband? Once you get help, you will have to determine the cutoff time that the cleaning must be done. If I have a weekend job now, I tell my staff that it must be cleaned no later than 7 pm on Saturday, this is an important decision, especially if your employee has an emergency. It will give you the owner extra time to clean the office before 6:00 am Monday.

NOTES

_____

_____

_____

_____

_____

_____

_____

_____

_____

_____

_____

_____

_____

14: BUSINESS MATERIALS NEEDED

Buy 3 x 5 index cards and use them to document all your phone calls.

Date:
Company Name:
Contact Name:
Address:
Phone:
Email:
Comments:

Always write the date on the card when you make additional calls to follow up with prospective customers.

Indicate all comments of the conversation.

When making a follow-up call, it is very important to read your previous written comments, before placing the call.

Purchase brightly-color paper to make flyers that will capture attention. An example of a flyer and letter to potential customers is provided at the end of this section. Be sure to change the company name and contact information.

Purchase White copier paper for your company stationery. You will need this white stationery when writing a cleaning proposal.

You can purchase an inexpensive computer or laptop at most big box stores. You also can reach out to a service to provide for you on an as-needed basis any documents you need to create. Lastly, the library will allow you to use their computer for free.

Printer/Fax (you can buy inexpensive two-in-one device versions at big box and discount stores usually for less than $75.00) These two-in-one devices give you the ability to print invoices, print estimated quotes, print scope of cleaning services, and also print flyers.

I recommend the faxing ability because you can fax your company flyer to hundreds of companies in place of walking from office to office handing out your flyers.

Ink cartridges (will be needed for the Printer)

You may also consider using phone apps that enable you to do all of the above.

A popular app option is to sign up with a great app called square. This app will enable you through your mobile phone to invoice your customers and accept your customers' credit cards for payments.

Business Cards (You can order these online for a reasonable price or call a local printer.)

Ledger Pad with a minimum of 4 columns can be used to maintain a log of all customer's outstanding and paid invoices. See ledger images below.

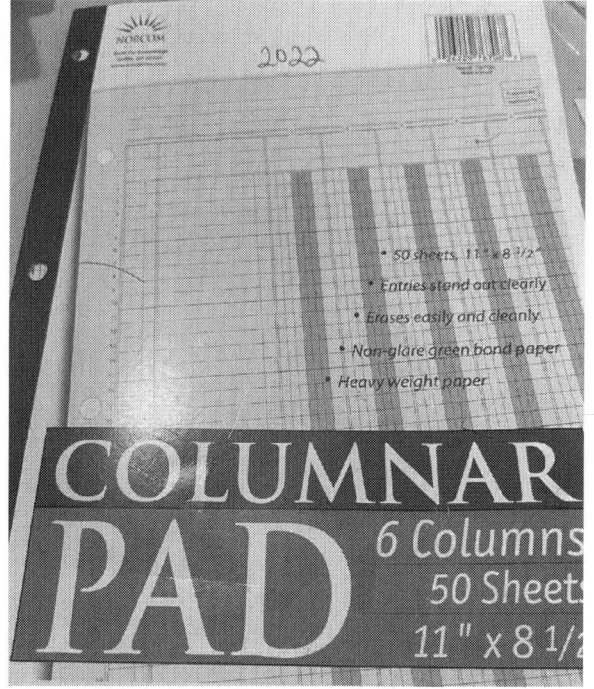

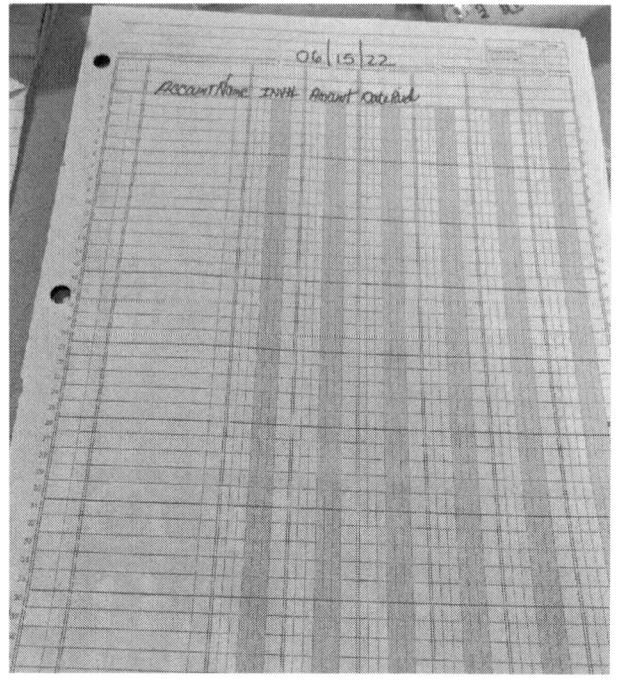

Use 8 ½ by 11 blank folders to maintain customer Information.

Use a 5 ½ by 4 inches notebook (to keep all incoming calls logged by the date received)
Paper clips

Pens & pencil (red pen to post payments received)

Scissors

Calendar

Inkpad with banking account for deposit only (you can get a customized one through your bank)

Colorful post-it note pad (comes in real handy to write quick reminder notes

Tape

Sample Flyer

A B C CLEANING COMPANY

 *Goode Cleaning Services*

*Check Picture Frames and Door Frames If You See **DUST**
Then Consider **Us**, We Don't Cut Corners We Clean Them*

NO CONTRACTS REQUIRED

CALL (888) 123-4567 OR (888) 123-4567

Licensed & Insured

DAILY • WEEKLY • MONTHLY

• VACUUMING	• POLISH FURNITURE
• SWEEPING	• RESTROOMS
• MOPPING	• LIGHT SWITCHES
• EMPTY TRASH	• KITCHEN/MICROWAVE
• DUSTING	• DOOR HANDLES
• CHAIRS	• CONFERENCE ROOM
• PICTURE FRAMES	• GLASS PARTITION
• SANITIZE TELEPHONES	• WIPE WINDOW SILLS
• FILE CABINETS	• FRONT DOOR GLASS
• DESK	• CLEAN MIRRORS
• WATER FOUNTAINS	• DUST LAMPS

Sample Letter to Potential New Customers

A B C CLEANING COMPANY

123 Address Line
City, FL 11111
(111) 111-1111

www.ABC.com
abs@gmail.com

Sample Letter to Potential New Customers

As a business owner, you spend a great deal of time and money developing a customer base. I am sure that you want to keep your current customers as well as get new customers.

When your customers walk through the door you should always want them to come into a nice clean office.

Offices that are dusty and not maintained clean are an eyesore. The last thing you want is for your customers to enter a dirty bathroom or dusty reception area, this lack of cleanness reflects on you the business owner.

We recommend the Cleaning of your office either weekly, bi-weekly, or at a minimum once a month. First impressions are lasting. The reception areas, the bathrooms, the examination rooms, the private office, or the conference room where you are meeting with a client. Keeping these areas cleaned at all times is what we help you do,

Call today for a free estimate of your office's cleaning needs.

Scope of Services Sample Letter

A B C CLEANING COMPANY

123 Address Line
City, FL 11111
(111) 111-1111

www.ABC.com
abs@gmail.com

To: Mrs. Smith, Manager
    Company Name
    123 Address Line
    City, ST 12345

Listed below is the scope of the services AB C Cleaning Company performs on a Deep Cleaning. The cost is $ _____

- Cob Web Cleaning throughout the entire building
- Ceiling Fans
- Blind Dusting
- Wall Light Switch Plates
- All Bathrooms are cleaned
- Front Entrance Glass Door
- Computer Room and all tables are dusted, and room is vacuumed
- Exercise Room Equipment is dusted, and floors are maintained
- All Glass Doors are cleaned

- Air Vents
- Chair Rails
- Bathroom Light Fixtures
- Entire Building Base Boards
- Sweep and Mop all floors
- Front and sitting reception areas are dusted, cleaned, and vacuumed
- Mail room is dusted
- Tenant Sitting Room tables are dusted, and room is vacuumed
- Library Room is dusted
- All floors are vacuumed
- Trash Rooms and Storage Rooms are swept and mopped

Any clarifications to the above, feel free to call me at the number above.
Your Name, Owner

NOTES

_____

_____

_____

_____

_____

_____

_____

_____

_____

_____

_____

_____

15: ADDITIONAL CUSTOMER INFORMAITON

I'd like to share an incident with you about a customer. I'll never forget when a new potential customer gave me their cleaning account. The client said that she selected me over all the others, even though I was new to cleaning because when explaining how I would clean, I mentioned that I disinfected the phones. To this day, I make sure all my cleaning staff disinfects our clients' phones. Today, because of COVID- 19, be sure to inform customers that as part of your regular cleaning you will always include disinfecting phones, light switches and all door handles., This should create an additional opportunity for a new client.

Some clients may only want you to clean their office during their 9 to 5 working hours. Often, they don't want to trust someone with a key. Other times they will want you to only clean during the weekend. Whatever day or time they request your cleaning services, if you do not want to lose the client, then you will have to clean during the requested time.. If this is your full-time job, this will not present any difficulties. However, if you start off the business on a part-time basis and you personally cannot clean, then you may have to hire someone to clean on your behalf. Sometimes you may be asked who will be doing the cleaning. Just be honest and say if it's you who is going to clean and if it's not you, then proudly say one of my employees.

I recommend you suggest the

cleaning of an office either weekly, bi-weekly or at a minimum once a month. Of course, if you are replacing a service ask what day they want you to clean.

NOTES

_____

_____

_____

_____

_____

_____

_____

_____

_____

_____

_____

_____

16: HOW-TO CLEANING TIPS

Information to help you navigate how to clean offices.

Left to Right Cleaning Method

Clean from left to right. This is a concept that will keep the level of your service high. Cleaning left to right is like reading a book; you don't start reading on the right side of the page and then read the left page. This left-to-right method will eliminate the possibility of missing different areas. More importantly, this procedure will ensure quality control on your part.

An easy way to assure the left-to-right method.

Walk into any room and, starting

at the left of the room work your way through the room. When you reach the end of the right side of the room you should be done with all the cleaning.

Desk

Sometimes a customer will request that under no circumstances you should clean a desk. You may also be told never to clean any and all desks. This request is not the norm but you should respect their wishes.

When wiping any desk carefully lift papers or any items like a stapler, pen, desk calendar, etc. Wipe the desk and immediately place the item EXACTLY where you found it. This will be the most important thing to learn when cleaning all desks. You do not want to get blamed for misplacing anything which may upset the client.

Pulling Trash

Trash cans are 90% of the time under the desk. When cleaning the desk pull the trash, and at the same time Always Follow this rule. This is part of the left-to-right procedure. Train anyone you hire to do it the same way. The reason why you should always use this method of pulling trash whenever and wherever the trash can is that if you don't do it when you first see the can, you can easily forget about it later. This is the number one customer complaint I receive.

In my experience always put several trash bags inside the can, this will help you not waste time looking for a bag when you are pulling the trash. Additionally, if you only clean the office bi-weekly or monthly the customer will appreciate your consideration by having trash bags in the can for their convenience.

IMPORTANT Note: When you clean any doctor's office or dentist's office never pull any trash in a RED bag. It's important not to pull this type of trash because the red biohazard bags have contagious or dangerous medical waste. All medical facilities hire special contractors to pick these bags up. You should never deposit anything else into these cans that have red bags for example paper or clips because it will cost your client money.

Computers

Do not touch Computers! This is important., Do not wipe the computer screens; however, it's okay to wipe the computer stand because they are usually black and collect lots of dust.

Chairs

After you clean a desk wipe the chair's arms and sitting cushion every visit. The chair legs can be done every two or three months.

Conference Room

Many offices have a conference room. Make sure you clean this room every cleaning visit. This room is used when clients come to visit. Don't forget to wipe the chair arms and cushions.

Window Sills

Always wipe the window sills in every office.

Kitchen

Many offices will have a small kitchen. below are item's to look out for. Remember to pull the kitchen trash.

Table

Wipe down and disinfect with an all-purpose cleaner.

Dishes

You may find a dirty cup or plate; as a courtesy, you can wash them for the client.

Microwave

Always spray an all-purpose cleaner to disinfect the inside to remove all food smells. Open the door and completely wipe the top, sides, bottom, and glass door inside and out. Always wash the glass turntable plate, even if it looks clean.

Kitchen Counters

Wipe with a disinfectant cleaner.

Sink

Wash the sink and if it's stainless steel, dry it very well and spray a stainless-steel cleaner on your rag and polish it.

Bathroom

Toilets

Disinfect toilets, wipe the seat on both sides, wipe the top of the tank, toilet base, and the toilet handle and never forget to wipe the bottom knobs on both sides.

Toilet Paper Holder

When toilet paper is pulled, it tends to leave a powdery residue on both sides of the holder and on top of the holder, a simple wipe will do.

Always make sure that the toilet paper holder has plenty of paper additionally leave two full rolls of toilet paper in all bathrooms.

Bathroom Sinks

Always do after you have cleaned the toilet and don't forget to wash the faucets then wipe them with a dry rag and they will shine.

Light Switch Plate

Always wipe down and disinfect.

Door Knobs

Always use a rag to wipe down

and disinfect.

Bathroom Mirror

Do this last. If you clean them first, I promise you will get water on it as you use the sink to wet your rag.

Sweeping

Always sweep the bathroom first before you start cleaning. Sweeping first will avoid the floors from getting wet as you wash and clean any area.

Mopping

This should be the last thing you do in all bathrooms.

Glass Front door

Use a rag to clean inside and out with a glass cleaner or plain water.

Glass Partition

Wipe on an as-needed basis and use a glass cleaner or plain water.

Vacuuming

After cleaning an area, then vacuum your way out of the room. When vacuuming, always lift up computer wires under the desk, with one hand gently lift up wires and with the other, vacuum under the desk.

NOTES

_____

_____

_____

_____

_____

_____

_____

_____

_____

_____

_____

_____

17: PRODUCTS AND SUPPLIES

Microfiber rags are highly recommended, buy them from discount stores or big box stores for the best prices. They are great for cleaning everything, desk, bathrooms, kitchen glass, etc.

A microfiber dust rag is a great thing to have as part of your cleaning supplies; this rag is good to use, dry damp or wet.

The microfiber rag is so effective that you can wet it, put stainless steel spray on it, or any disinfectant or furniture polish on the rag, and use it to clean any and all hard surfaces. Always wash microfiber rags with bleach to disinfect them.

4 Empty spray bottles are a

necessity to have in your cleaning business there are multiple uses for spray bottles.

1 - Use one for bleach, and always put a plastic disposable glove over the spray squirt because you can spill some as you walk from one area to the next Use the bleach for toilet bowls that are bad and or sinks.

2 - Use multi-purpose cleaners and disinfectants. There are many to choose from.

3 - Use a floor cleaner with a lavender scent. Put a cap full into your water bucket and ring the mop well. You can use this lavender scent on hard floors and tiles. This lavender fragrance will become your signature trademark, it smells wonderful. If you use too much, the floors will become sticky and the fragrance will be too strong. (Do not

use the lavender liquid on wood floors. Only use products specifically made for wood floors).

4 - Glass cleaner or plain water can be used for mirrors, glass doors, etc.

Other supplies:

- Pumice Stone (use for stains in toilet bowls)
- Disposable Gloves
- Furniture Polish
- Powdered cleanser
- Stainless steel cleaner (use for stainless steel sinks and stainless steel refrigerators). Spray directly on the rag, not on the appliance.
- Hand Sanitizer - keep in your car. Use after each office cleaning.
- Vacuum
- Broom

- Mop
- Dust Pan
- Bucket for mopping
- Toilet Brush / Toilet Brush Holder

Floor machine. You can purchase a floor machine for less than $100 at a big box store, but I do not recommend that you do this in the beginning. Wait until you get an account that has a lot of floor work. A floor machine is lightweight and does a great job, and you can use it in place of a broom.

Plastic Caddy case to hold your spray bottles and cleaning products.

NOTES

_____

_____

_____

_____

_____

_____

_____

_____

_____

_____

_____

_____

18: BILLING/INVOICES

Your clients will almost never pay you at the time you clean their office. Most companies will require you to submit an invoice. Get in the habit of consistently creating your invoices on the 15th and 30th of every month and email your invoices to save postage.

Purchase a ledger pad. Examples are provided in Chapter 14: Business Materials Needed. You can find one in any office supply area of big box stores. Make sure whichever one you choose has four columns.

This will become invaluable to you. Tracking how your money comes in is important. You can receive a check in the mail, then go straight to the bank and deposit it.

However, if you don't post the payment, you will forget who paid and when they paid you. It will be embarrassing to call a customer for payment and have them tell you that the check was sent out two weeks ago. If you do not keep track of who has paid and who has not, you will become an inefficient record keeper, (and lose money!).

As your customer base grows, you will see the value of this simple billing system.

Keep receipts for all expenditures, i.e., cleaning products.

Get 8 ½ by 11 gold envelopes. Label the outside of the envelope with your company name and month and year. Put all your purchased receipts and bank statements for the current month inside. At the end of each month, you just close the envelope and give it to the bookkeeper or accountant.

A B C CLEANING COMPANY

123 Address Line
City, FL 11111
(111) 111-1111

www.ABC.com
abs@gmail.com

DUE UPON RECEIPT

Date: _____

INVOICE # 8030
To: **XYZ Company**
  222 Address Line
  Suite 111
  Any City, State 11111

DESCRIPTION OF CHARGE:	**AMOUNT**
1 Office Cleaning Friday 06/15/20	$75 per cleaning

TOTAL AMOUNT DUE: $75.00
(add % tax, if applicable $)   5.25 tax

TOTAL $80.25

After 5 days pay $87.75

MAKE CHECKS PAYABLE TO ABC CLEANING
Net due upon receipt. All balances not paid within
5 days of invoice date will be subject to a 10% late fee

NOTES

_____

_____

_____

_____

_____

_____

_____

_____

_____

_____

_____

_____

19: SALES TAX

As a business, you must charge Sales Tax. By law, you only have to collect the Sales tax for office cleaning, never for home cleaning. You must report and PAY the total sales of the previous month to your state's sales tax department each month. Check with your local state department for when the tax is due. In my state of Florida, all sales tax collected must be turned in to the state by the 20th of each month for the previous month. Sample ledger sheet on the appendix page.

The ledger book should have items listed below:
Example
December 15, 2021
December 30, 2021

- 1st column customer's name
- 2nd column invoice number (keep progressing invoice number
- 3rd Column total (do not include tax in the total amount
- 4th column date invoice is paid

Add all the amounts from column 3 for the 15th & 30th.

At the end of the month, tally all your amounts for the entire month, write the total and multiply the total by your state's tax percentage, e.g., 7.5%.

Example: Total for the entire month $1000.00, multiply by 7.5% total amount you collected would be $75.00. That is the amount of sales tax you are responsible for paying to the department of revenue in your state no later than the 20th of every month.

You may want to consider a free digital invoicing system that generates reports.

NOTES

_____

_____

_____

_____

_____

_____

_____

_____

_____

_____

_____

_____

20: NETWORKING

It's my job to pass the baton and share what I know about networking. Networking is an inexpensive and effective marketing tool to develop new business. This method of marketing can replace radio advertising and newspaper ads.

Most companies require their managers to attend either daily or weekly staff meetings. As an employee, you have no choice but to be present in these meetings. As a business owner, you need to invest time in as many network groups as you can. In the same way managers were obligated to attend staff meetings, you need to sacrifice some of your time to grow your very own business. Do not consider networking a chore. View it as a great opportunity to speed up the growth of your new business.

When I started my cleaning company, I knew absolutely nothing about networking. One day someone invited me to a networking meeting called BNI, a national networking organization. I went to the meeting early in the morning, and it was one of the best business decisions I ever made for the growth of my company.

Networking is an important marketing tool that most cleaning companies do not take advantage of. Networking is a process that enables you to meet and develop relationships with other business owners.

You can search online for networking meetings in your local

area.

I recommend you start with the Chamber of Commerce. They usually have several groups known as councils that meet throughout the month. When you attend any network group rule # 1 is to bring business cards. You should never leave home without your business card.

Most meetings will encourage you to arrive 15 minutes earlier, and this is a great business practice you need to adhere to. Arriving early helps you to warm up and to start meeting and talking to others. Once the meeting begins, the host of the meeting may ask first-time visitors to stand and introduce themselves. This is your opportunity to say your name, your company name, and thank the person who invited you to the meeting. Some networking groups allow each person about one minute to speak about their business. When it's your turn to speak again, here is a sample you are welcome to use:

Hello, my name is John Smith, owner of ABC Company. We clean offices, we don't require that you sign a contract, and our rates are affordable. Use us weekly, bi-weekly, monthly, or on an as-needed basis.

John Smith with ABC Company
(The next line say very slow for an impact.)

WE DON'T CUT CORNERS WE CLEAN THEM.

This is what is known as a tagline it makes your company memorable.

This is called a 1-minute spiel - it's precise and to the point. I have perfected it to about 23 seconds. Don't speak too fast you have plenty of time. Allow your audience in the meeting, whether in person or in a virtual meeting, to clearly hear:

- Who you are
- Your company name
- What you do
- How inexpensive your service is (mentioning affordable is a clue)
- And by saying your tagline slowly, Mine is:
  - (We Don't Cut Corners We Clean Them
- Creates an unforgettable Tagline

A Tagline is a closing statement that you will be remembered by.

Networking meetings are

normally 1 hour long and the most popular starting times are 7:30 am, 8:00 am or 8:30 am.   The early starting time is to give business owners the opportunity to attend the meetings and get to work no later than 9.30 am.   Some networking groups have luncheons or early evening social meetings.

The   number   one   rule   of networking is "People like doing business with who they know, who they like, and who they can trust.". This important lesson will propel you to increased business. When you attend the various networking events be on the lookout for certain types   of   business   that   can complement your cleaning business, such as home services like:

- Carpet Cleaning
- Electricians
- Exterminators

- Lawn Service
- Painter's
- Plumbers
- Real Estate Agents
- Window Cleaning

These businesses are known as power leads because the owners of them have already made connections with their clients. Developing a relationship with these business owners will become the vehicle that will help you propel your business growth. You will certainly meet many other business owners at the various networking events and meetings that you attend.

Understanding the One-on-One Rule

The previous statement that "People will do business with people they know and whom they like and can trust" start with what is known as one-on-ones. One-on-ones are meetings that you have with other business owners who attend the networking events you go to. These can be brief phone appointments, online meetings, or in-person appointments that enable you both to speak for a few minutes about your business. You will then have the opportunity to get to know one another a little better. Feel free to allow your guest to speak first. Take the time to tell them about your family, your company, and very importantly ask how you can give them a referral. The objective is not to necessarily to do business with one another, but **through** each other by giving one another future referrals.

When you attend any networking event, first listen for the names of the power lead companies listed above. Write down their names when you hear them speak, at the end of the meeting walk over introduce yourself, and request their business card. If you are meeting through a virtual meeting save the chat room information. In about a day or two, call the person and request a phone or in-person appointment.

This is the beginning of developing a relationship that will help you know more about the individual and their business. The objective is to convey how you can be of help to them in the referral process.

If you currently have a day job and are going to clean offices in the evening or if you are shy and don't feel comfortable personally engaging with speaking and meeting others, you may consider asking someone to represent you.

There are many stay-at-home moms and you can interview some right in your local neighborhood, or you can consider a well-spoken friend or relative to represent you at the networking meetings. Offer whomever you select an hourly rate ($10 for example) to represent your company at the various meetings.

Create an inexpensive business card from a local or online printer for this individual with their name, your company name, and your phone number. By putting your phone number on their card, when someone calls asking for her you can immediately identify where the caller heard of your company.

NOTES

_____

_____

_____

_____

_____

_____

_____

_____

_____

_____

_____

_____

_____

21: POWER 2 CHANGE

Congratulations on making this great investment both in yourself and your new cleaning company. You will discover that you will get out of this investment whatever you put into it. The power 2 change is the catalyst that you already have because you have stepped out on faith to become a great entrepreneur.

Power 2 change is a mindset that you have to utilize daily. It will begin every morning when you make phone calls, the will not to make phone calls will come through your mind and you need the internal power of wanting to succeed over not wanting to make phone calls.

The mindset of thinking positive when you make a phone call is critical, every call you make you must believe that this could be the call that they will say yes, they need your service.

Power 2 change is making a deliberate conscious effort to do and think only things that can help you succeed. Don't give energy to thoughts that are not empowering to you, this is a daily ritual that you must adhere to.

Power 2 change is a great inward feeling this monumental sensation is what you will need forever, feelings are the route feelings are everything in a nutshell. Try to visualize what you want in your future don't forget to add feelings to those wonderful goals.

As you embark on starting your

cleaning service remember to set yourself up for success, develop a daily call list of 25 minimum phone calls, the will to not make phone calls will come through your mind and you need the internal power of wanting to succeed over not wanting to make phone calls.

The mindset of thinking positive when you make a phone call is monumental, every call you make you must believe that this could be the call that they will say yes they need your service.

Whenever you feel like quitting, remember why you bought this manual, remember the feeling you had when you made the decision to own your own company.

Power 2 change is comprised of a spirit of gratitude get in the habit of being thankful, being appreciative of all the small things and all the big things that will follow.

There are many lessons you will learn on your own but one of the most important lessons I want to share is "there is enough business for everyone."

In 2008 when my company Goode's Cleaning was nominated small business leader of the year, I had a long registration questionnaire to fill out. One of the questions was, "how do I feel about my competition." I said to my husband Andy, "wow, this next question is a really hard one." When I repeated the question, he answered why do you think it's hard since there is enough business to go around for everyone.

I answered him by saying there are more than over 1,000

companies in Jacksonville; how are you going to say there is enough to go around for everyone? Andy pointed out that there are over tens of thousands of companies and only thousands of cleaning companies. This smart revelation full of pure wisdom became a huge inspiration for me.

I want each and every one of you to read the following statement listed below and to carry this great knowledge forevermore, may God bless you to understand the value of this great truth.

God's great abundance is in the sky, your eyes can never see all the sky in the entire world at one time.

God's great abundance is in the ocean, your eyes can never ever see all the water in the entire world at one time.

God's great abundance is in the tree's you can never ever count the leaves in any one tree, the leaves in just one tree are so many just imagine every tree on this planet you just can't count them.

And last but not least, God's great abundance is in every blade of grass. Just imagine trying to count all the blades of grass in the world; totally impossible.

Well, all the examples above are here to encourage you that the sky is your limit, remember God's great abundance is here for you as well. You have taken the first step in becoming self-independent Never give up on yourself do not allow a no to determine your future and know that if I could build my cleaning company from scratch so can you. My email for consultations and

coaching   is
goodescleaning@comcast.net.

Congratulations on starting your own Office Cleaning Business!

NOTES

_____

_____

_____

_____

_____

_____

_____

_____

_____

_____

_____

_____

22: CUSTOMERS FREQUENTLY ASKED QUESTIONS

While many of your questions will be answered in detail as you read the book, you may have a few questions that you want answered right away. Provided in this chapter are questions often asked.

Customer: Do I have to sign a contract?

Answer: No, we require a 30-day mutual termination agreement.

Customer: How do I pay you?

Answer: I will invoice you on the 15th and 30th of every month via email. You can make your check payable to Blank Company.

Customer: Are you insured?

Answer: Yes, we are licensed, insured, and bonded.

Customer: Who will clean the office?

Answer: Myself or one of my employees.

Customer: Will the same person clean my office each time?

Answer: Yes, the same person will come every time.

Customer: Do we have to provide our own cleaning supplies?

Answer: No, we provide the products.

Customer: Do you supply paper

products?

Answer: No, you are responsible to provide all paper products, trash bags, toilet paper, and paper towels.

Customer: When will the cleaning be done?

Answer: A staff member will come between 6 pm Friday through Sunday midnight.

Questions You May Be Thinking About

At this point, you're probably thinking that yes, I have money to commit to starting this business and yes, I don't mind cleaning. Now what?

You're probably wondering, without experience, some of the

following:

- How can I get customers?
- How can I learn to clean professionally?
- I want to be the boss, but I don't want to clean myself.
- What products do I need?
- What office supplies do I buy?
- Where do I go to get my business license?
- How much should I charge?
- How do I get paid?
- What time do I start cleaning?

I know the questions in your head keep coming, but relax; that's why you invested in this cleaning manual.

NOTES

_____

_____

_____

_____

_____

_____

_____

_____

_____

_____

_____

_____

_____

Made in the USA
Columbia, SC
26 September 2023

23268904R00076